The Tree & Me

A Polyvagal Poem

WRITTEN BY **Katy Dickson**

ILLUSTRATED BY **Regan and Alexis Desautels Cruz**

AUTHOR'S DEDICATION

For Esme, my daughter, my reasons, my roots.
For Sally, my sister, my counsel, my anchor.

HARDCOVER ISBN: 978-1-954332-55-3
SOFTCOVER ISBN: 978-1-954332-56-0
Library of Congress Control Number: 2024940497

© 2024 Katy Dickson. All rights reserved.
Artwork © Regan Desautels and Alexis Cruz Gomez.

Wyatt-Mackenzie Publishing
DEADWOOD, OREGON

The tree and me love to feel free,

My heart on my face for all to see,

Branches outstretched shouting look at me!

It is so much fun to be carefree.

My roots deep down in the ground below,

With strong foundations I reach out and grow.

The tree and me just want to be free,
Yet always we are connected, the wide world and me,
To earth, tree others, to myself, within.
Through this, my journey of safety does begin.
Many seasons to embrace, their gifts to unfold,
I will face many challenges as I grow old,

But with the sound of sweet lullabies whistling in the breeze,
I go about my business with awe and ease.
And as water and sunshine nourish my soul
I learn a dance with life to keep me whole.

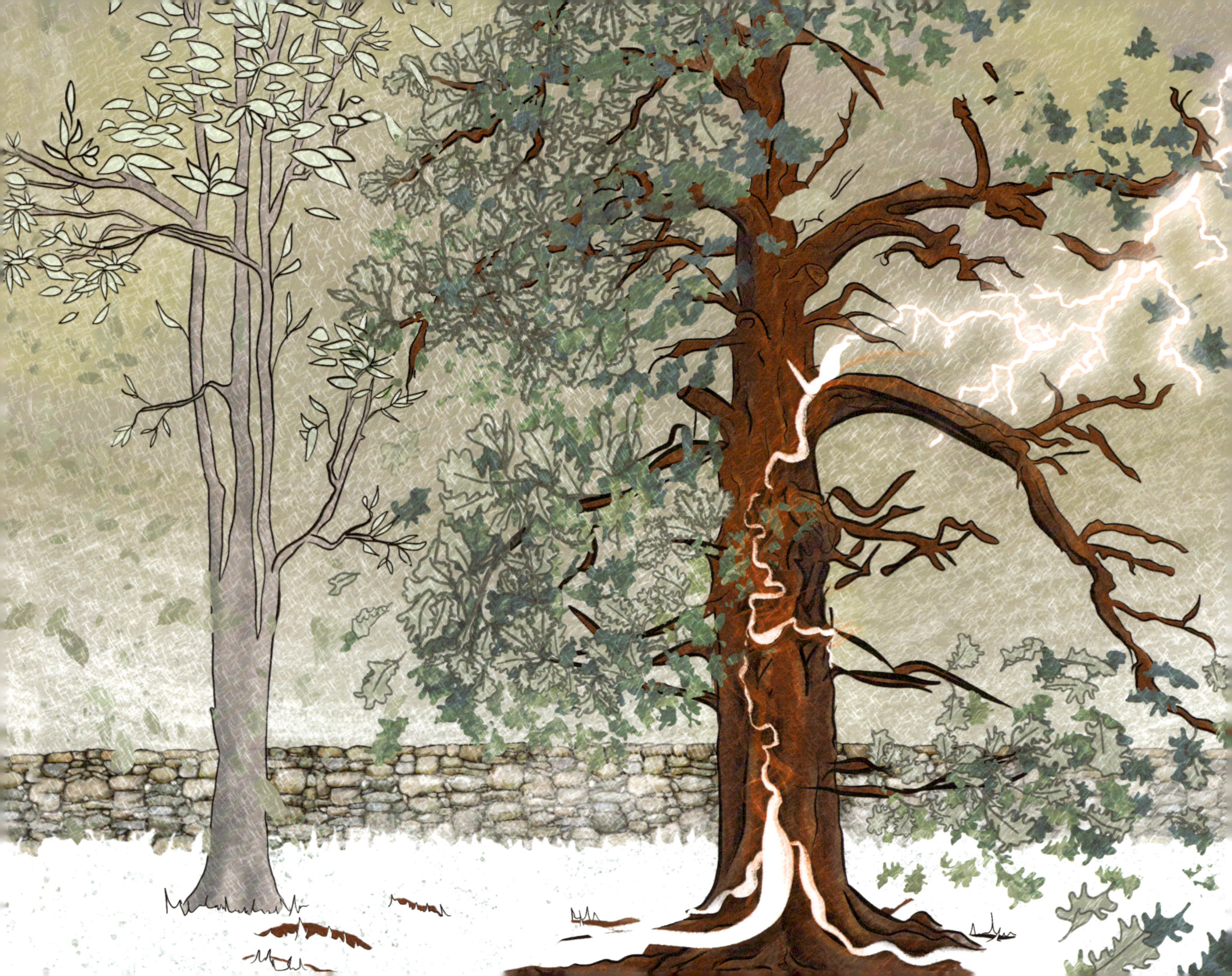

The tree and me love to feel free,
But sometimes the lightning, it frightens me,
It strikes at my bark and twists my insides,
I am hurt and scared but there is nowhere to hide.

My heart has started to thump and pound,
I cannot seem to hear another sound.
My focus is gone, except this need to survive,
My body has gone into automatic drive.
Only anxiety and anger are left inside,
It's like I am a runaway train ride.
I am distracted, jumpy, I'm breathing fast, too.

Does any of this feel familiar to you?
Sometimes it's hard to know what to do.

But the tree and me just want to be free

So, I find a way to come back to me.

I press pause, slow things right down,

Anchor my roots way down in the ground.

Then I peek inside for what I need,

And breathe deep to my tummy until at last I am freed.

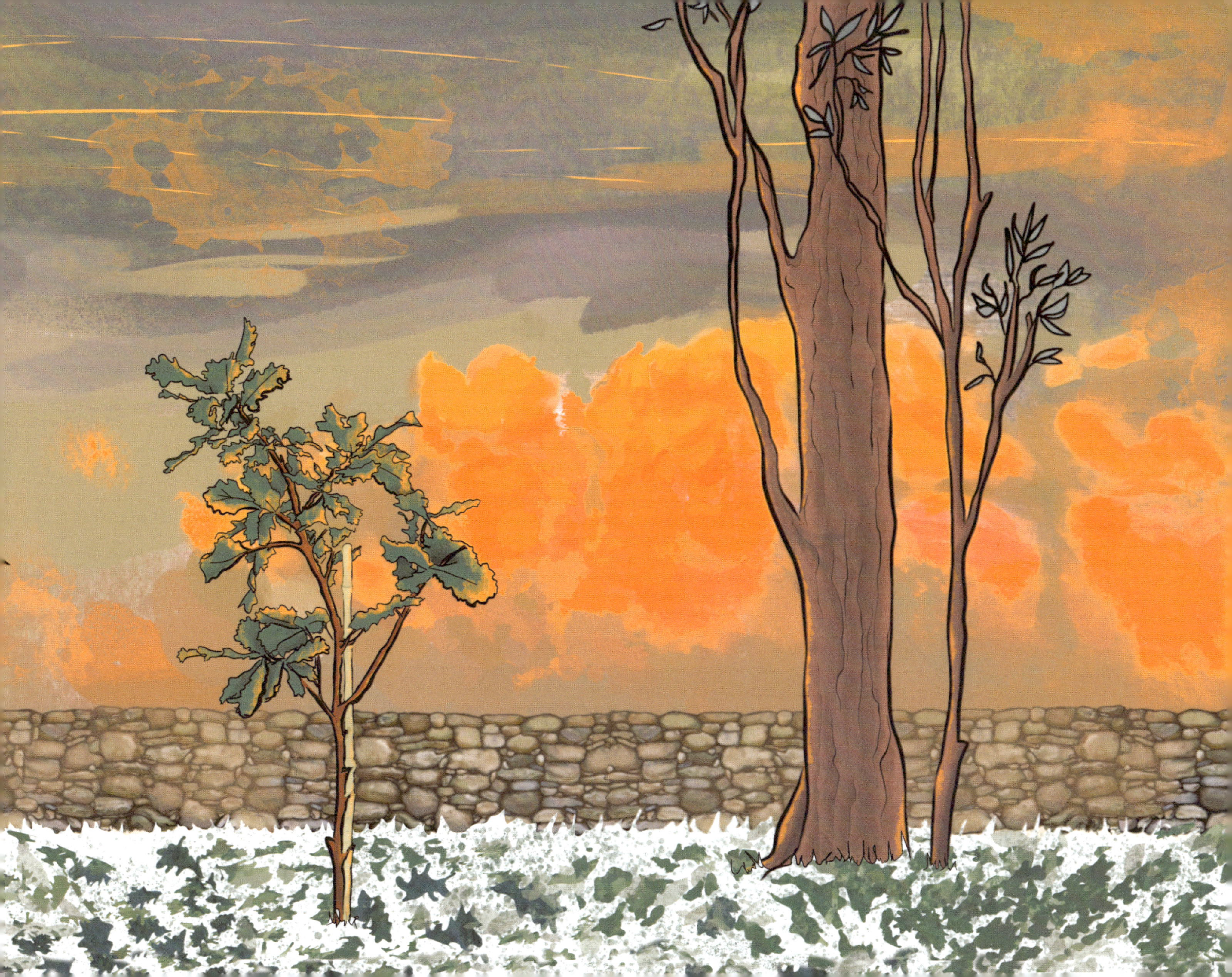

The tree and me love to feel free,

But sometimes the wind, it won't let me be

It pushes me this way, it pulls me that,

It tugs at my leaves, bending the twigs right back.

My body takes over,

My brain's out of sight,

Only two options available run or fight?

All I can hear is the blood in my veins,

Nothing even looks the same.

Unfamiliar faces all around,

Voices now just a distorted sound.

I cannot find a safe connection,

All that is left is self-protection,

I am frightened, worried, it's chaos inside…

How did I get back on this runaway train ride?

Does any of this feel familiar to you?
Sometimes it's hard to know what to do.

But the tree and me to just want to be free

So I find a way to come back to me.

I rise with its bluster yet anchor my roots,

This strengthens my trunk but gives flight to my shoots.

I can move around more flexibly,

But never stray too far from me.

I practice letting go of what has been said,

Write down how I feel so it doesn't live in my head.

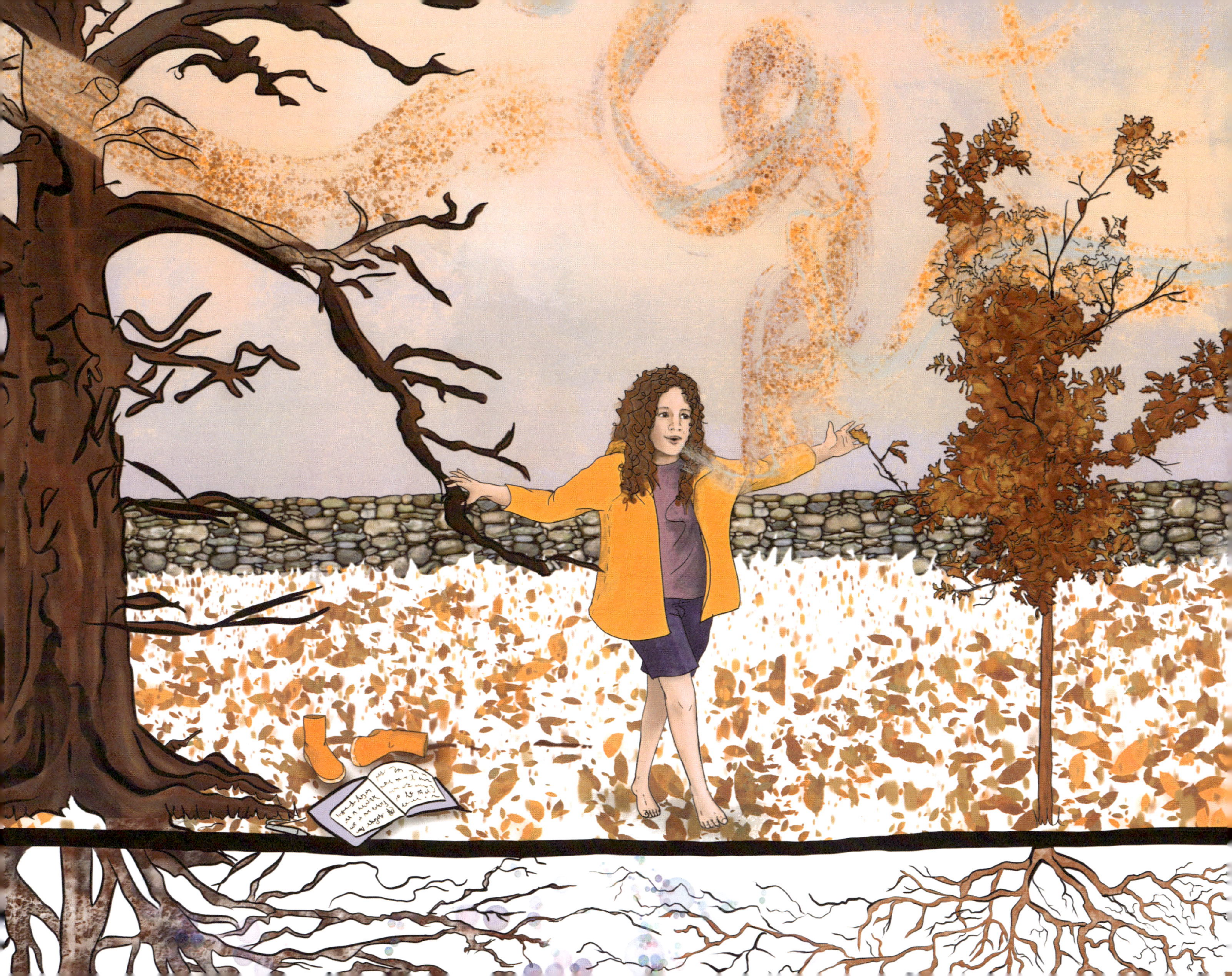

The tree and me love to feel free
But sometimes the darkness, it overwhelms me,
I surrender to stillness, suspended in freeze.
No sound of sweet lullabies whistling in the breeze.

I can't feel my body, where is my head?
I don't even remember the last thing that I said.
Please can I curl back up in my bed?
What is the point of all this?
I feel heavy, lost, in the abyss,
I am no use here, there is no hope,
Such feelings of shame, I cannot cope.
With the world spinning in slow motion,
I sit here alone, in endless procrastination.
I feel so small, not connected at all.
My heart is quiet, my breath shallow, too.

Does any of this feel familiar to you?
Sometimes it's hard to know what to do.

But the tree and me just want to be free,
So, I find a way to come back to me.
I search for starlight in every direction.
Sense out safe trees for kindness and connection.
A gentle rock, invite some energy back,
Movement will get me back on track.
Find some laughter, engage in play.
These help to keep the darkness at bay.

I also think, it's worth a mention,
That we have at our fingertips, life's greatest invention.
A hug, a squidge, a snuggle, a squeeze,
Although, always ask permission from your fellow trees.
And if no other passes in the breeze,
Then you hold yourself tightly until you feel a release.
This is one of the best things you can do,
If the opportunity is available to you
Ask the universe for that loving cuddle,
Guaranteed to soothe many a muddle.
And the great thing is, it doesn't just help you,
But it can feel pretty good for the other, too.

The tree and me love to feel free

But sometimes with all that life can be

There is a whisper 'danger' but no threat in front of me

I may start to feel I want to run or fight

Or I may just want to curl up and hide

I have all those feelings that I did earlier describe

But everything is happening deep inside.

It's like it's not me who gets to decide.

Does any of this feel familiar to you?
Sometimes it's hard to know what to do.

But the tree and me just want to be free,

So I find a way to come back to me.

I learn about what it means to 'be,'

And how my body responds to take care of me.

I thank it from the bottom of my heart.

In the race of life, it's given me a head start.

I take note of how my insides feel,

And what about me this might it reveal,

Where I am in a moment in time,

Then out from this place I can gently climb.

My breath and movement support me along

So, I do not get stuck in fight/flight or shutdown for too long.

I make friends with my biological brilliance,

This will help to scaffold a healthy resilience.

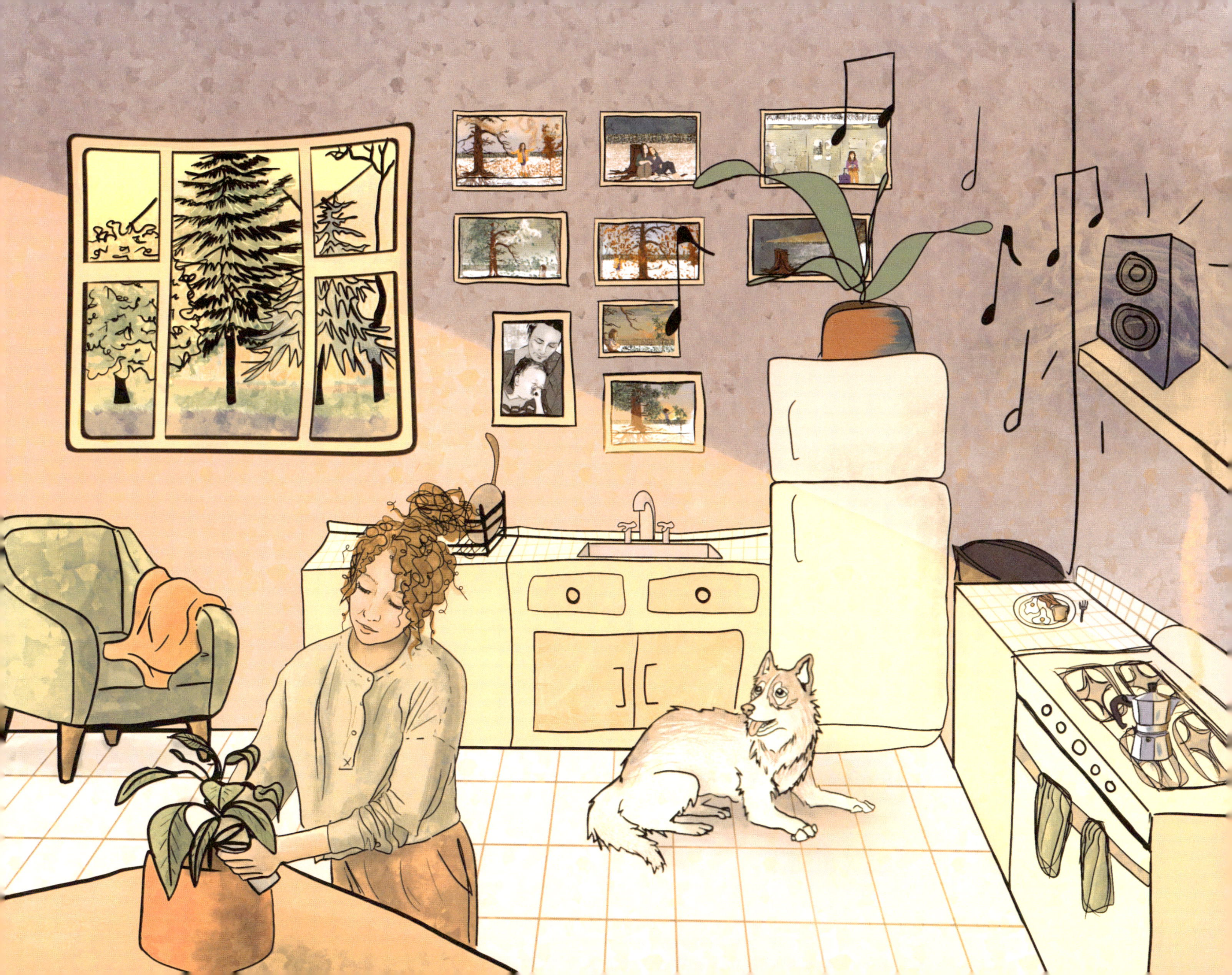

The tree and me love to feel free,

My heart on my face for all to see.

Branches outstretched shouting look at me!

It is so much fun to be carefree.

My roots deep down in the ground below

With strong foundations I reach out and grow.

The tree and me just want to be free,
Yet always we are connected, the wide world and me,
To earth, tree others, to myself, within.
Through this, my journey of safety does begin.
Many seasons to embrace, their gifts to unfold,
I will face many challenges as I grow old,

But with the sound of sweet lullabies whistling in the breeze,
I go about my business with awe and ease.
And as water and sunshine nourish my soul
I dance in life and celebrate I am whole.

How *The Tree & Me* Came To Be

The Tree & Me emerged during a time of healing. What began as a personal endeavour to explore embodied ways to be free of the impact of trauma, later ignited a deep resonating passion to understand more about trauma's application, not only to self but also to others.

This particular chapter in author Katy Dickson's life began in 2020 while she was training to be a TRE Provider. During a class, Dr. David Berceli talked about Dr. Stephen Porges' Polyvagal Theory. *It was as if a light had been switched on!*

To gain greater understanding, Katy first studied to become a Safe and Sound Protocol (SSP) Provider and then, under the expert provision of Dr. Liz Charles, embarked upon her own SSP adventure as a client. Through learning about trauma and the nervous system response, she felt able to take back control of her life. An aspect of this work was her reconnection with writing, wordsmithery, and poetry, an art of self-expression previously enjoyed that had been temporarily lost in the shadows.

Inspired by this process, Katy would often write poems between sessions and share her creative work. Excited by "The Tree & Me," Dr. Charles shared it with Karen Onderko who kindly arranged for a private reading with her and the other Polyvagal Institute Founding Members: Dr. Stephen Porges, Deb Dana, and Randall Redfield. From that "once in a lifetime" moment, she was delighted to be invited to debut "The Tree & Me" at the first Polyvagal Summit in November 2021. The response received from delegates and the "call to action" to publish was both humbling and overwhelming.

A further opportunity arose to share her work on a global platform when Katy was approached by Joao Marcal-Grilo, Founding Director of Jaya Mental Health; he invited her to open a webinar for the Nursing Now Challenge "Nursing in Conflict" and recite her poem as a "seed of hope."

Sometime later, like the roots of a tree laying further foundations, Randall introduced Katy to Dr. Lori Desautels, Butler University, who invited Katy to open her classes with "The Tree & Me," and this in turn led to the serendipitous connection with Regan and Alexis.

Katy has long standing roots in Occupational Therapy (OT). Currently specialising in the field of Paediatrics she is a Principal Therapist, a primitive reflex integration practitioner and trauma informed. Integrating her "lived experience," the Polyvagal "lens" and the diverse practices of her professional life extending beyond OT, TRE, and SSP to ayurvedic abdominal massage and fascial unwinding, she began to deliver a blend of uniquely attuned interventions at her private clinic. Katy went on to empower others sharing her poem as a therapeutic tool.

Living in the leafy green suburbs of southeast London, Katy leads a full and busy life. She is passionate about getting out into nature with her mischievous puppy, Maggie. She is fortunate to be surrounded by many wonderful friends and is raising an amazing human, who defeated the odds and provides daily inspiration.

Thanks & Acknowledgements

To my family, special mention to my mum, dad, and sister aka Brenda, John, Sally and "G" and Aunty Chris, who have been by my side throughout all the seasons and helped me to navigate to safety through the lightning, the wind, and the darkness with their unconditional love and unwavering support. Thank you for being my team. I love you.

I am truly blessed to have very dear and special friends in my life: you know who you are! Thank you for believing in me and giving me courage to get out there and celebrate my work. You are the best kind of people. I love you.

Respectfully and with thanks to Dr. Liz Charles and in deep gratitude to the Founding Members of the Polyvagal Institute, Dr. Stephen Porges, Deb Dana, Randall Redfield, and Karen Onderko, for their ongoing support of my creative work, the generosity of their guidance and direction, and for providing safety in abundance within which this seed was able to flourish.

Dr. Lori Desautels, thank you for being a positive light throughout and for the vivacity of your spirit and belief in the poem.

To two incredible humans, Regan & Alexis, for being my "partners in rhyme"! For the soulfulness, the time and energy, the joy and deep resonance you bring, this connection has been a spiritual one. I am so very grateful to have had the opportunity to feel this in my lifetime, to collaborate with you has been so special. Your art is incredible, thank you for breathing life into my poem. How exciting to share our book with the world.

A massive thank you to Alisa Conan for sky diving into my life, courtesy of a timely and stunning introduction from the one and only Laura Sierra, Osteopath and human extraordinaire, and to all of your team; special mention to Lou and Coralina, you all so beautifully crafted a safe vessel for me to be me.

To the courageous souls who put their trust in me to provide safety and a compass as they embarked upon their own healing process and for embracing Polyvagal Theory as a guiding light. It was an honour to journey with you.

With thanks to Madeline Fox for her brilliant, massive legal brain!

Full appreciation to Ruth Veda for your giving nature and for connecting me with Sat Dharam; to you I express my deep gratitude and respect for the generosity of your time and support through the sharing of your poignant, expert insights.

Where would we be without our brilliant publisher Nancy: we have danced every conceivable dance with you throughout this whole experience! Wow, what an adventure. It has been nothing short of incredible. Thank you so much for your expert guidance and for making "two" dreams come true.

Katy

The Illustrators

Regan and Alexis Desautels Cruz are partners in life and in their artistic work; the *Tree & Me* is the third book they have co-illustrated.

Alexis is a graphic designer from Hermosillo, Hidalgo Mexico. He has previously worked for local organizations Saberes Indigenas (Indigenous Wisdoms) and ALIDMEX ~ Alianza Indígena Para el Desarrollo de México (Indigenous Alliance for the Development of Mexico), and international organizations SlowFood and Revelations in Education. Regan is from Indianapolis, Indiana, and her educational background is in human development, psychology and peace, justice, and conflict studies. She has both taught and worked in the education field as a graphic designer and learner experience designer at New Teacher Center and at Revelations in Education. The two met, fell in love, and began collaborating after Regan's Fulbright scholarship led her to teaching in Hidalgo, Mexico.

This creative team is passionate about highlighting the work of activists, educators, and thought leaders by making it visual, interactive, and accessible to the masses and everyday change makers. It has been the gift of a lifetime to bring out another dimension in Katy's masterpiece, and they are honored to have been able to co-create at her side. Alexis and Regan's other shared works include illustrations in *Intentional Neuroplasticity: Moving Our Nervous Systems and Educational System Toward Post-Traumatic Growth* and *Body and Brain Brilliance: A Manual to Cultivate Awareness and Practices for Our Nervous Systems.*

Afterword

written by
Stephen W. Porges, Ph.D.
CREATOR OF THE POLYVAGAL THEORY AND CO-FOUNDER OF THE POLYVAGAL INSTITUTE

The Tree & Me offers a profound reflection on Polyvagal Theory's principles through its evocative language and imagery. The line, "Yet always we are connected, the wide world and me, to earth, tree others, to myself, within," speaks directly to the theory's concept that our sense of safety and well-being is deeply intertwined with our relationships and environment. This interconnectedness is essential in regulating our autonomic states, reinforcing the idea that we are not isolated beings but part of a larger, interdependent system.

The poem continues with, "Through this, my journey of safety does begin," which mirrors the journey outlined in Polyvagal Theory, where our autonomic nervous system shifts between states of safety and defense. This journey towards a state of calm and social engagement is a fundamental aspect of finding peace and stability. The poem beautifully captures this transition, highlighting the importance of feeling safe to fully engage with others and the world around us.

Reflecting on, "Many seasons to embrace, their gifts to unfold, I will face many challenges as I grow old," we see a parallel to the dynamic nature of our autonomic states. Just as our nervous system adapts to various challenges and experiences, we too must embrace change and growth throughout our lives. This acceptance and learning from life's seasons contribute to achieving a regulated and balanced state, a core tenet of Polyvagal Theory.

Finally, the line, "And as water and sunshine nourish my soul I dance in life and celebrate I am whole," encapsulates the essence of Polyvagal Theory. Positive experiences and connections nourish our nervous system, fostering a sense of wholeness and well-being. Feeling safe and connected allows us to thrive and fully engage with life, celebrating our wholeness.

The Tree & Me elegantly captures the essence of Polyvagal Theory by highlighting the importance of connection, safety, and nurturing experiences in achieving a state of well-being and wholeness. The poem serves as a beautiful reminder of the profound impact of our relationships and environment on our mental and physical health.

www.ingramcontent.com/pod-product-compliance
Ingram Content Group UK Ltd.
Pitfield, Milton Keynes, MK11 3LW, UK
UKRC031958280425
457979UK00001B/1